WIRE MILL DAM FISHERY

This dam is full of fish and d[...] summer months maggot or swe[...] catch all day long. Great for bee[...] plenty of roach. perch, tench, [...] head of crucian carp. There ar[...] large carp, well into double figu[...]

quality roach and perch also makes this water one of the best winter fishing venues in the area.

Fish-it2

Published by:
Arc Publishing and Print
166 Knowle Lane
Sheffield S11 9SJ

Produced By: Chris Keeling

2 for 1
DAY TICKET VOUCHER

Allows 2 anglers to fish for the price of a full adult day ticket.

To be signed by
Wire Mill Dam Fishery bailiff

....

ISBN: 978-1-906722-10-4

ACKNOWLEDGEMENTS

I would like to thank the following for their
help in producing this guide:
South Yorkshire Tourism for the use of their map.
Doncaster & District Angling Association.
Denaby Miners Welfare A.C.
Clive Nuttall secretary of Catcliffe, Treeton Anglers Alliance.
All fishery owners and angling clubs who have kindly
provided information.

August 2009

Arc Publishing and Print
166 Knowle Lane
Sheffield
S11 9SJ

W E L C O M E

Like many other anglers, my time on the bank is limited, but I like to grab a few hours fishing whenever and wherever I can. Always bearing this in mind, I have put together this third edition of 'Fish-it 2 South Yorkshire'. I have included details of some new venues in the area, and have updated all the best day ticket waters from the previous edition, many of which I have fished and caught well and others where I struggled but still managed the odd fish.

I have included photographs, price details, directions and maps, rules for each water and type of fish stocked.

Fishing attracts so many people. Perhaps it is the solitude in often beautiful surroundings. Of course there is also the eager anticipation of catching a big one! The bank side can be almost hypnotic and the desire to catch just one more fish has spoilt many a meal.

I hope you find this book useful and wish you good luck, good fishing and remember - "A bad day's fishing is still better than a good day's work!"

Chris Keeling

C O N T E N T S

A B O U T   T H I S   G U I D E

To help you locate a fishery, the venues have been arranged
in alphabetical order and split into two sections, fisheries
and rivers. Their approximate location has been indicated on
a map on page 8, 9, 10 & 70.

Green Section   Fisheries

Brown Section   Rivers

Each page contains details of a fishery,
with information on the following:

Ticket Price:	All day ticket costs plus details on OAPs, disabled and junior concessions.
Directions:	Usually from the nearest city or town, or from the closest motorway junction.
Description:	A brief outline of what the fishery looks like plus details on features such as islands, depths and the best places to fish.
Types of Fish:	List of species present, many with estimated weights.
Rules/Bans:	The restrictions set by the fishery on type of baits, hooks etc.
Number of Lakes:	The number of waters available to fish at the venue.
Facilities:	What is available at each location i.e. cafe.
Telephone:	The number of either the owner, angling club secretary or match organiser.
Sat Nav:	Post Codes for use on satellite navigation systems.

S P E C I E S / S Y M B O L S

Most commonly found in
the South Yorkshire area.

 BARBEL

 BREAM

 CARP

 CHUB

 CRUCIAN

 IDE

 ORFE

 PERCH

 PIKE

 ROACH

 RUDD

TENCH

TROUT

 Camping

 Caravan Site

 Drinks

 Disabled Access

 Toilets

 Food

 Parking

 DACE

 GUDGEON

 Location of fishery on Section Maps

To help you find the nearest
place to get tackle and bait,
you will find a list of fishing
tackle shops in South
Yorkshire on page 78

P O L E   F I S H I N G
F O R   T H E   B E G I N N E R

Of all the different methods of fishing I've tried, I haven't found any of them as accurate or as easy as pole fishing. To be able to place your bait and feed to the exact spot, sometimes only inches from an island or group of reeds is what makes pole fishing so productive and fun.

T A C K L E   N E E D E D

A Pole

Poles come in various sizes, from 4 metres (usually called a whip) to poles of 18.5 metres. They also vary dramatically in price as well, this is usually governed by weight and rigidity. The lighter and straighter (no droop at the end) the more expensive they are. I recommend a pole between 11 and 13 metres, stay away from the smaller telescopic ones. Many tackle shops have poles ready assembled for you to handle, make sure you are comfortable with its weight and it feels well balanced. Test that it takes apart smoothly. If possible, get a pole with a spare top section as they enable you to rig up for different species and size of fish.

Pole Rigs

Experienced anglers can make up their own pole rigs but beginners are advised to buy ready-made. There are plenty of quality ready made rigs available for as little as £2.99. These rigs come with a main line with a loop on the end (used to attach the line to the stonfo connector at the tip of your pole). A float with enough shot below it to cock it nicely in the water and a length of lower breaking strain line, which has a spade end hook tied to it. The float and shot can slide down the line and be adjusted accordingly.

Pole Elastic

The elastic that runs through the top sections of your pole cushions the fight of a hooked fish and allows you to play it. Elastics are graded in sizes 1-20.
The following list is a good guide for the beginner:
1. For small roach and perch for example - use a No4 elastic with a 1lb hook length and a 2lb main line.
2. If fishing for small carp and tench or skimmer bream use a No8 or 10 elastic with a 3.5lb main line and 2.5lb hook length.
3. When fishing for carp up to 12lbs use a No16 to 18 elastic, and a main line of 8lb with a 6.5lb hook length.

S T A R T   T O   F I S H

Fishing Position

Get your seatbox in position. Ideally, when sitting on the box, your thighs should be in a horizontal position, at right angles to your lower leg. Holding the pole correctly makes it comfortable for long periods and prevents backache. For a right handed person you need to rest the pole across your knees with your left hand supporting it. Put your right forearm along the end of the pole and firmly grip the pole with your right hand. Have close to hand - your bait, landing net, disgorger and anything else you may require for your days fishing. It is important to have your pole roller in the correct location. The pole has to be well balanced in your hands when it leaves the roller - this prevents rig tangles when shipping out.

Start Fishing

You have set up your pole and plumbed your depth - so now you are ready to fish. Make sure you have between 10" and 20" of line between the tip and float. In more windy conditions you may want to lengthen this. Feed your swim with groundbait (if allowed) plus a few bits of your hook bait. This is more accurately done using a pole cup which can be fixed to the end of your pole. Put your bait on the hook and ship out your pole trying to keep your rig in the water as this prevents tangles. Lay the rig on the water lengthways. The shot on the line will pull the line under the water and cock the float.
Enjoy your first pole fishing day!

7

SOUTH WEST OF BARNSLEY, ROTHERHAM AND SHEFFIELD

8

BARNSLEY TO THE
NORTH OF DONCASTER

Motorway
A Road
B Road
Other Road
Railway
Trans Pennine Trail

○ Village
○ Small Town
○ Medium Town
□ Large Town
□ City

③ Motorway Junction
Ⓢ Service Area
▲ Mountain Peak

EAST AND SOUTH OF DONCASTER

Map courtesy of South Yorkshire Tourism,
which is a project part-financed by the
European Union, European Regional
Development Fund, through Objective 1.

Motorway	○ Village	③ Motorway Junction
A Road	○ Small Town	Ⓢ Service Area
B Road	○ Medium Town	▲ Mountain Peak
Other Road	☐ Large Town	
Railway	☐ City	
Trans Pennine Trail		

Abbeydale Dam

Abbeydale Industrial Hamlet
Abbeydale Road South, Sheffield.

Ticket Price: Day ticket £5.00 (£4.00 after 4pm)
Available from Woodseats Angling Shop.

Directions: From the centre of Sheffield take the A621
(Abbeydale Road). After about 3 miles go straight on at the
traffic lights at Beauchief. The Dam is 300 yards on your left
just after the Hamlet entrance.

Description: This well run water is between 4 and 5 acres in
size. The depth varies from the dam wall end at around 20
feet to a foot deep at the far end. The 10 day ticket pegs
which are next to the road are an ideal depth of between 5
and 6 feet. Fishing is very good from any of these pegs with
the dominant species being rudd and tench. This is not a
carp lake so don't expect to be snapped by a twenty
pounder. The bank next to the railway line is for season
permit holders only, contact the bailiff for details.

Types of Fish: Bream, tench, roach, rudd and crucian carp.

Rules/Bans: Barbless hooks, no groundbait, no meats,
no boilies, no night fishing.

Number of Lakes: One

Facilities: None   **Sat Nav:** S7 2QW

Telephone: 0114 2589578 or 0779 2657669

Aston Park Fisheries.

Aston Ponds, Mansfield Rd, Aston, Sheffield.

Ticket Price: Day tickets are £5.00, Concessions at £4.00.

Directions: From junction 31 of the M1, take the A57 towards Sheffield, at the first roundabout turn left heading towards Killamarsh. Turn left after a few metres and follow the lane to the ponds.

Description: All pegs at this large four pond fishery are new and many are suitable for anglers with disabilities. The waters have plenty of bankside features to target. You are spoiled for choice with so many good pegs to chose from, but you can't go wrong fishing for carp with some luncheon meat on the Lily Pond. Stable Pond is also well worth a try as that too has plenty of large carp present. Lanta Pond is packed with fish but smaller and is more suited to the novice angler.

Types of Fish: This water has large stocks of silver fish, with roach and perch to a good size. Stable Pond has been stocked heavily with carp. Bream and chub feature to 4lb with roach and perch to just over 2lb. There are some very big carp to over 30lb.

Rules/Bans:

ASTON PARK FISHERIES
RULES

- BARBLESS HOOKS ONLY (MAXIMUM SIZE 12)
- NO BOLT RIGS OR FIXED FEEDERS
- 2 KEEP NETS TO BE USED FROM APRIL-NOV
- KEEP NETS ONLY TO BE USED IN MATCHES
- NO TINS ON BANK
- 2KG GROUNDBAIT (MAX)
- 1KG WORM, JOKER & BLOODWORM
- 1 TIN OF CAT MEAT (400g) PER DAY
- NO NUTS
- NO NIGHT FISHING
- NO FLOATING POLE IN MATCHES
- MAXIMUM POLE LENGTH 16 METRES
- GROUNDBAIT TO BE CUPPED IN OR THROUGH FEEDER
- 1 ROD PER DAY TICKET
- NO BRAIDED LINES
- ONLY ASTON PARK FISHERIES FEED PELLETS TO BE USED FOR FEED

ALL EXCESS BAIT & LITTER TO BE REMOVED FROM SITE
THESE RULES ARE TO PROTECT THE FISH & FISHERS

Number of Lakes: Four, with three more being built.

16

Facilities:

Telephone: Alex 07743 845737

Sat Nav: S26 5PQ to the industrial units near by.

Aston Springs

Aston Ponds, Mansfield Rd, Aston, Sheffield.

Ticket Price: Day ticket £5.00. OAPs £4.00 Mon-Fri
Year permits £65.00 which includes KJS and West End
Fisheries (13 ponds in total).

Directions: From junction 31 of the M1, take the A57 towards
Sheffield. At the roundabout turn left heading towards
Killamarsh. Turn left after a few metres and follow the lane
to the ponds.

Description: Ponds 1 and 2 formerly known previously as
Laycocks Ponds are the first ponds you see. The three
newly built ponds are on your right and have been stocked
with a variety of fish and are already fishing well. Lake 2 has
a good head of bream and some big carp to 27lb. The
newly built platforms are excellent to fish from, plus the new
cafe is very reasonable.

Types of Fish: Carp up to 27lb, bream, roach, ide, chub,
rudd, and barbel.

Rules/Bans: Barbless hooks only, keepnets in matches only.
No ground bait except in pole cup or feeder.

Number of Lakes: Five

Sat Nav: S26 5PQ to the industrial units near by.

Facilities:

Telephone: 0114 2470876

13

Bank End Fishery

Bank End Road, Finningley, Doncaster.

Ticket Price: Day tickets £5.00 Concessions at £4.00.

Directions: Take the A614 to Blaxton. When you come to the crossroads with the Blue Bell pub, turn right onto the B1396. The waters are on the righthand side.

Description: Bank End has three lakes, the newest being a 34 peg match lake which is stocked mainly with carp. The other two lakes of about 4 and 3 acres are open all year round. The excellent shop which sells locally produced goods has a cafe where you purchase day tickets. Most of the 120 pegs are suitable for anglers with disabilities. I prefer the smaller of the two lakes as it's more sheltered. I did well fishing close to some reeds with a 5 metre pole.

Types of Fish: Plenty of roach, perch, and rudd. There is also quite a few Chub present. The Skimmer bream are now reaching a good size. Loads of carp too.

Rules/Bans: No dogs or radios permitted. No carp in keepnets, no bloodworm, hemp or tares. No Ground bait, barbless hooks only.

Telephone: 01302 770224

Number of Lakes: Three

Sat Nav: DN9 3NT

Facilities:

 62

Barlow Fishery

Barlow Trout and Coarse Fishery, Barlow.

Ticket Price: Coarse day ticket £5.00 After 1pm £4.00 Juniors, OAP's £4.00. Evening tickets £3.00.
Matches by arrangement.
Trout Lakes: Full day £14.00 four fish taken. Six Hours £12.00 three fish taken. Six Hours £10.00 two fish taken.

Directions: The fishery is located in the village of Barlow on the B6051, midway between Chesterfield and Owler Bar. Look out for the signs at the west end of the village.

Description: A great fishery for all ages and abilities with the last of the four lakes being most suitable for beginners. This well established fishery gives the angler plenty of choice with four coarse lakes and four trout lakes, plus a small brook. The four coarse lakes are stocked with a variety of fish with the largest carp being in the first two waters. The third pond is the tench pond and the last one is mixed. The cafe serves a great bacon sandwich.

Types of Fish: Carp, rudd, bream, tench, roach, trout, barbel, and chub.

Rules/Bans: Barbless hooks only , no keepnets, no hard baits, no ground bait, no hemp.

Number of Lakes: Four coarse, four trout.   Sat Nav: S18 7TJ

Facilities:

Telephone: 0114 2890543

Barnburgh Lakes

Ludwell Hill, Barnburgh, Doncaster.

Ticket Price: Day Tickets £5.00. Concession £4.00.

Directions: From junction 37 A1(M) take Barnsley Road A635 towards Barnsley. Take your third left onto Blacksmiths Lane. Continue down this lane until you reach a T junction. Turn right onto Ludwell Hill, you will see the fishery about half a mile on your left.

Description: This disabled friendly new fishery has only been open a year and a half but is already fishing well. Now the third lake is open it has a total of 82 pegs. Depths are between 2 and 3 metres with and island in one lake to fish upto. Most pegs have been designed that you can park behind them. Although very new there are some good sized carp present, a few reaching 18-20lb.

Types of Fish: Carp. Bream, Barbel, tench, rudd and roach.

Rules/Bans: All Nets must be dipped on site, Keep nets to be used in matches only, Barbless Hooks only Max size 14. Barnburgh feed pellets only. No Boilies, No Trout Pellets, No Cat or Dog Meat, No Nuts.No Floating Poles or Floating Baits including Bread. Ground bait only in cup or feeder. No litter to be left. No dogs, radios or wading.
All under 16's must be accompanied by an Adult.

Number of Lakes: Three   Sat Nav: DN5 7EE

Facilities:

 46

Telephone: 07714 765 488 or 07752 528 086

16

Bradleys Ponds

Geer Lane, Ford, Sheffield.

SAT NAV S12 3YH

Ticket Price: Day ticket £5.00. £3.00 after 4pm

Directions: From the A6102 Sheffield ring road at Gleadless turn onto White Lane signposted Mosborough. After a mile turn right to Ridgeway. Follow the road till you reach Ford. Turn left after the pub on the corner and continue up Geer Lane until you reach the farm. The ponds are on your left.

Description: There are three ponds to try. I prefer the middle one which is also the largest at around two acres.
This pond has a small island at one end which I fished up to using a 13 metre pole. I caught a few carp at an average weight of 8lb + plenty of silver fish. This is a popular fishery so it is advised to arrive early to get a good peg, the fishing is also much better early on at Bradleys. Set in an attractive valley of a working farm.

Types of Fish: Carp, bream, tench, perch, roach and rudd.

Rules/Bans: No carp in keepnets, No cereal ground baits except bread punch, barbless hooks only. No dogs.
No night fishing.

Number of Lakes: Three   **Sat Nav:** S12 3YH

Facilities: P

Telephone: 01246 435563

Bolton Brickponds

Furlong Road, Goldthorpe, Bolton-upon-Dearne.

Ticket Price: Day tickets £3.00. Multi rods £6.00. Concessions £1.50, Multi £3.00. Year permits are available, ask the bailiff

Directions: Come out of Barnsley on the A635 heading towards Doncaster and turn off when you see a sign for Goldthorpe (B6098). Turn off right and follow the road through Goldthorpe and after a mile you will see the ponds on your left.

Description: There are 3 inter-connected ponds to fish and with water around 28 foot in places, it's great for all year round fishing. There is plenty of different swims to fish and a lot of open grass areas for picnics. Most pegs are accessible to disabled anglers. Their are some huge carp in these waters, so make sure you take some heavy tackle if thats what you aim to catch.

Types of Fish: There are the occasional tench up to 8lb. Bream to 7lb, pike to 26lb, rudd, roach and crucian to 2lb. Carp well over 20lbs. Plus a few chub.

Rules/Bans: No keepnets, barbless hooks only. Permit required for night fishing

Facilities: **Number of Lakes:** Three

Telephone: N/A   **Sat Nav:** S63 9PT

39

18

Candy Corner Fisheries

Wroot Road, Finningley, Doncaster.

Ticket Price: Day tickets £5.00 Concessions at £4.00 Fishing from 7.30 am till 7.30pm.
Now open all year.

Directions: From Doncaster take the A638 to Bawtry and follow the signs for Auckley. Turn left onto the B1396. Straight over at the roundabout in Auckley then take the first left signposted Wroot. After about a mile you come to the water on your left, just before a sharp bend.

Description: There are 4 lakes to fish at this venue. The largest water is known as AJ's and has 45 pegs with a depth of around six feet. Hoskers Lake which is smaller has 26 pegs and is also shallower, about five feet. This fishery is stocked with a mixture of quality fish but the carp seem to be the dominant species. This water is very well kept and most pegs are suitable for disabled anglers.

Types of Fish: Carp running to over 30lb. Bream and tench to 9lb and 6lb. The rest of the stock is made up of roach, perch, rudd and ide.

Sat Nav: DN9 3DZ

Rules/Bans:

Candy Corner Fisheries Rules
1. Barbless hooks only
2. Maximum hook size 12
3. Keepnets only allowed in matches
4. No bloodworm or jokers
5. No boilies or trout pellets
6. The only pellets allowed are our own which can be purchased from bailiff on site (only one bag of each per visit)
7. No method feeder
8. No seed baits to be used
9. Ground bait in feeder or pole cups only
10. Maximum pole length 13 metres
11. No time i.e. Corn or meat to be taken onto this fishery
12. No dogs
13. Under 16's must be accompanied by a adult at all times
14. All nets to be dipped
15. Do not discard unwanted bait into lake. It must be taken away
16. Anyone found fishing with barbed hooks will be asked to leave
17. Regular hook checks will be carried out
18. Landing nets to be used at all times i.e. Landing and returning of fish

Thank you!
HAVE A GOOD DAYS FISHING

NOTICE
All nets to be dipped before commencing fishing

Number of Lakes: Four

Facilities:

Telephone: 01302 775062

Carterhall Fishery

Carterhall Lane, Charnock Hall, Sheffield.

Ticket Price: Day ticket £4.00 Concessions £3.00

Directions: Turn off the A6102, Sheffield ring road and head towards Ridgeway on the B6388. Take the third right turn into Carterhall Road. Turn left just after the school and follow the lane down to the farm. Look for the fishing sign.

Description: This fishery has matured nicely but is still only five years old. There are only 20 concrete pegs so come early at weekends to get a good one, peg one never fails!. It has two islands to target and a depth of around five feet. The bankside planting has now grown adding more features to target. This is a clean, well run fishery. Luncheon meat hair-rigged with a small amount of ground bait in a feeder works very well between the islands.

Types of Fish: Carp up to 23lb, bream to 3lb, tench to 4lb perch to 2lb. Other species include roach, orfe, ide, chub, rudd, and barbel.

Rules/Bans: Barbless hooks only, no keepnets. No cat or dog food.

Number of Lakes: One   **Sat Nav:** S12 3XD

Facilities:

Telephone: 0114 2815483 mob 07718 512958

Cow Gap Farm Pond

Hill Top Road, Stannington, Sheffield.

Ticket Price: Day tickets £5.00. Concessions £4.00.

Directions: Head out of Sheffield on the B6077 Loxley Road. Take your next left after the Admiral Rodney public house. After 2 miles turn left into Lee Moor Lane. Follow to the T junction and turn right. After 300 yards turn left onto Hill Top Road. Follow the road until you see the fishery on your right.

Description: This small twenty peg pond has a huge variety of fish species for its size. The anglers who could reach the corners of the island in the middle were catching well using sweetcorn or pellet. I managed to catch plenty of rudd and ide close to the reed bed margins. There is very little shelter at Cow Gap and the wind can be viscous, but don't let that put you off, its well worth a visit.

Types of Fish: Carp reach 12lb, bream to 6lb, tench to 4lb. Roach, rudd, chub, ide, barbel and crucian carp are all present.

Rules/Bans: Barbless hooks only. No boilies. Groundbait in moderation. No meat as or in groundbait. No cat or dog food. No keepnets except in matches.

Number of Lakes: One   **Sat Nav:** S6 6GW

Facilities: 🚻 🅿 ♿   Caravan and campsite very close by. 20

Telephone: 0114 2345234

Crookes Valley Park Lake

Crookes Valley Road, Crookesmoor, Sheffield.

Ticket Price: Free

Directions: From the centre of Sheffield, take the A57 Manchester Road. You will see signs for the university. At the university roundabout, take the third exit, which is Bolsover Street. Follow this road until you come to Winter Street and then onto Crookes Valley Road, you will see the park on your left hand side.

Description: This water covers just over 3 acres and has a concrete path all the way round providing plenty of places to fish. Depths vary all over this lake and in some places it is very deep, just under 30ft. Around the steps seems to be the most popular area to fish. It is rumoured that a 6ft catfish patrols the depths!

Types of Fish: There are plenty of carp in this lake and a few run up to 28lbs. Quality roach and perch are present, the larger ones approaching 2lb. Bream up to 3lb. There's also a few large chub nearing the 7lb mark.

Rules/Bans: No night fishing, no keepnets.
Park bylaws apply.

Number of Lakes: One   **Sat Nav:** S10 1BA

Facilities:

Telephone: Sheffield Council

Damflask Reservoir

Dam Flask Reservoir, Sheffield.

SAT S6 6HW NAV

Ticket Price: Adults £4.30. £3.20 for disabled, OAPs, and under 16s. Tickets purchased from a machine in the car park.

Directions: From Sheffield take the A57 towards Manchester. Then take the B6077 Loxley Road towards Bradfield, when you see the dam wall turn left.

Description: Situated about 7 miles outside Sheffield, it covers 115 acres, so if you like your solitude while fishing this water is for you. There is a road that runs the full way around the reservoir making access from your car easy. The water has a wide variety of depths with about six feet at the inlet to almost 100 feet at the dam wall, but the majority of the water averages between 15 and 20 feet. Damflask is a renowned pike venue and gives excellent sport especially in the winter months.

Types of Fish: Bream averaging 2 to 3lb. Chub up to 6lb and perch to 4lb. A few tench and roach can be found. Pike run to around 34lb.

Rules/Bans: No keepnets, no ground bait, no night fishing, no live baits.

Sat Nav: S6 6HW

Number of Lakes: One

Facilities:

 14

Telephone: 07952 485798

Dearne Valley Park Lake

Pontefract Road, Barnsley.

Ticket Price: Day ticket £2.00 Concessions £1.00
Year Ticket - £15.00 Adult, £7.50 Concessions

Directions: From the centre of Barnsley take the A628
Pontefract Road. After a couple of miles you will see a
pub called the Old White Bear on your left hand side. Take
the second turning on the left and follow down to the lake.

Description: Run by Hoyle Mill Angling Club this lake is a
perfect depth for the pleasure angler at just over 4 feet in
most places except for the odd trench going to about 6
foot. You can only fish the bigger of the two lakes as the
smaller one is for breeding. Using a feeder is the best tactic
to catch the larger carp nearer the two islands, but many
anglers were catching silver fish using a pole.

Types of Fish: Carp around 20lb mark, plenty of roach, perch,
chub, tench and bream.

Rules/Bans: No rods are to be left unattended. Only 1 rod
per angler. Barbless Hooks. No keepnets (only in matches)
No tents or night fishing. No Nuts, Peas, Beans, Boilies,
Blood Worm & Joker, Floating Baits, Spinners, Livebaiting.

Number of Lakes: One

Facilities:

Sat Nav: S71 1UH
to the pub near by.

Telephone: 01226 213686 or 07977 317085
Hoyle Mill Angling Club.

24

Delves Ponds, Thorne

Selby Road, Thorne.

Ticket Price: £3.00 a day. £2.00 concessions.

Directions: From Junction 6 of the M18 head towards Thorne on the A614. Once you have passed the railway bridge look out for the fishery on the right.

Description: A really good fishery to try with two lakes and plenty of features to target. Both lakes are stocked with most species and of about the same depth, around 7 feet at the deepest. However, I prefer the smaller of the two, fishing close to the island and catching every time. Roach and perch mainly but I had a couple of tench out. I think the larger lake does seem to be more for the carp angler.
These ponds caters for both the novice angler and the more experienced pleasure fisherman. Ideal baits are maggot and caster for the roach and perch or meat for the carp.

Types of Fish: Perch, roach, tench, bream, ide, carp and eel

Rules/Bans: Keepnets in matches only, barbless hooks only. No bloodworm or joker. No nuts or wasp grub.

Number of Lakes: Two   **Sat Nav:** DN8 4BH

Facilities:

Telephone: 01405 817294

Elm Tree Farm Fisheries

1 Elm Tree Farm Court, Hooton Roberts.

Ticket Price: £4.50, £3.00 after 3.00 pm,
£3.50 for under 15's and disabled. Matches £5.00

Directions: Take the A630 from Conisbrough to Rotherham.
When you reach Hooton Roberts take a right turn on to the
B6090. You will see the lakes on your left.

Description: This venue consists of two lakes. The smaller of
the two has 21 pegs and is called Hooton Hollows. It is a
well-established lake having been there for only 10 years.
The depth is about 6 feet throughout and will fish well at
most times of the year. The second larger lake is called
Horseshoe Lake and has over 40 pegs to choose from.
Both lakes are full of silver fish and armed with some
maggots you can't fail to catch, making this an excellent
venue for the pleasure angler.

Types of Fish: There are crucian to just under 3lbs. Carp can
reach 20lbs, but most average around the 3lb mark. There
are also plenty of chub and tench present between
4 and 5lb. Roach and perch to nearly 2lbs.

Rules/Bans: Barbless hooks only, no keepnets.

Number of Lakes: Two

Facilities: A small selection
of baits are sold
in the cafe.

38

Telephone: 01709 855219   **Sat Nav:** S65 4TE

26

Ferryboat Farm Fisheries

Ferryboat Lane, Old Denaby, Doncaster.

Ticket Price: Day tickets £5.00.

Directions: From the A1 Junction 36 take the A630 to Conisbrough. At the traffic lights turn right and head towards Mexborough on the A6023. When you reach a small roundabout, go straight over. Take the second turning on the left, signposted to Old Denaby. When you reach the village, turn right onto Ferryboat Lane, keep going till you reach the fishery.

Description: This four acre lake offers a good selection of 69 pegs with plenty of room between them. There are now caravan and camping facilities on site, great for a long stay. The water depth is between 5-6 feet which is ideal for the many carp in here, some reaching 15lb in weight.
Don't forget the reed margins as many good sized tench can be caught on sweetcorn or meat.

Types of Fish: The carp are mainly around the 4lb mark. There are plenty of roach, perch and rudd. Some very good tench can be caught in this lake, around the 9lb mark. Bream and chub are also present.

Number of Lakes: One

Facilities:

Rules/Bans: Barbless Hooks only. No Keepnets. See notice board as you drive in.

Sat Nav: DN12 4LB

Telephone: 01709 588088 or 07930 958605

Fleets Dam
Smithies Lane, Barnsley.

Ticket Price: Day Tickets £6.00. Concessions £5.00.
Year Ticket £80.00 Concessions £60.00

Directions: Take the A61 from Barnsley heading towards
Wakefield. After about a mile take a left turn into Smithies
Lane. Follow the road to the bottom of the hill and the dam
is on the left hand side.

Description: The depth varies a lot on this water which
favours the all year round angler. The bank closest to the
car park is the shallowest at just over 4 feet. There is also a
feature of a sunken wall about half way up the lake. This
can often be one of the better places to fish. This dam is
around 10 acres and has 75 pegs to choose from.

Types of Fish: Carp to about 17lb, but roach and bream are
the main species here. There's a few chub and plenty of
tench present, plus the odd pike in the mid twenties.

Rules/Bans: Barbless hooks only, no boilies or nuts.

Number of Lakes: One   **Sat Nav:** S71 1NL

Facilities:

Telephone: 01226 292579

28

Grange Farm Lake

Pinfold Lane, Fosterhouses, Doncaster.

Ticket Price: Day tickets at £5.00.

Directions: Leave the M18 at Junction 6, and head east towards Stainforth. Follow the signs for Fishlake, the farm is signposted from the road.

Description: This lake is now a few years old and is getting better all the time. It has 40 pegs and is very well stocked with a variety of species, making this lake ideal for the beginner to catch nets full of fish. Feeding a little and often with maggot or caster is your best bet. The small island and bankside features offer plenty of areas to target. This is a very popular well run fishery which can get busy so arrive as early as possible and check that there is not a match on.

Types of Fish: There are plenty of carp, with a few larger ones into double figures. There is a good stock of tench, roach, chub and bream.

Rules/Bans: Barbless hooks only, no cat or dog meat, no boilies, nut, or trout pellets. Children under 16 must be supervised.

Number of Lakes: One   **Sat Nav:** DN7 5LD

Facilities:

43

Telephone: 01302 846163

29

Harlesthorpe Dam

Rotherham Road, Clowne.

SAT S43 4PS NAV

Ticket Price: Smaller pond £5.00. Concessions £4.00 Large Dam £6.00. Concessions £5.00. Extra Rod £1.00. Night fishing on island only, £15.00 ring for details.

Directions: From the M1 take the A619 to Clowne. At the crossroad in the centre of Clowne turn left onto the A618. The fishery is a few hundred yards, on both sides of the road.

Description: The main lake of about 10 acres is mainly stocked with carp up to 25lb, and with plenty over 10lb you are sure of good net weights. The depth can vary from 5 feet in the reeds to 14 feet in the middle. I prefer the smaller lake across the road that is surrounded by trees and has a variety of fish present, with good sized chub and tench.

Types of Fish: Carp, tench, chub, roach, bream, perch, rudd and crucian carp.

Rules/Bans: Barbless hooks only. Children under 16 years of age must be accompanied by an adult. No dogs or radios permitted. Carp over 3lb exempt from keep nets (except for matches). No method feeder. No dog or cat meat allowed. Ground bait in pole or cup feeder only.

Facilities: ♿ P **Sat Nav:** S43 4PS 52

Telephone: 01246 810231 **Number of Lakes:** Two

Hayfield Fishing Lakes

Hayfield Lane, Auckley, Doncaster.

Ticket Price: Day Tickets £5 per peg. £6 per match peg, 7am till dusk.

Directions:

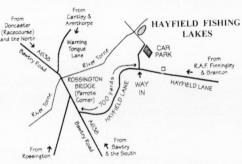

From Doncaster (Racecourse) and the North
From Cantley & Armthorpe
HAYFIELD FISHING LAKES
Bawtry Road
A638
Warning Tongue Lane
River Torne
River Torne
CAR PARK
From R.A.F. Finningley & Branton
ROSSINGTON BRIDGE (Parrots Corner)
700 yards
HAYFIELD LANE
WAY IN
HAYFIELD LANE
A638
Bawtry Road
From Rossington
From Bawtry & the South

Description: Hayfield Lakes are situated to the south of Doncaster in idyllic countryside, just south of Rossington Bridge. There are two large lakes; Adams Lake 82 pegs and Island Lake 79 pegs. A good days fishing can be had float fishing soft pellet, corn or maggot but use some small pellet feed to keep the fish in your swim.

Types of Fish: Stocked with carp to 32lb, ide and tench that reach 7lb, perch to 3lb, plus some large chub. Plenty of crucians, bream, roach and rudd.

Rules/Bans: No keepnets (except during matches) No night fishing. No barbed hooks. No hooks larger than a size 10. No dogs, litter, fires. No boilies.

58

Number of Lakes: Two   **Telephone:** 01302 864555

Facilities: Sat Nav: DN9 3NP

Horseshoe Lake

Forge Road, Wales, Sheffield.

Ticket Price: Day Tickets £5.00. (Tues-Sun) 7am till dusk.

Directions: Leave Sheffield on the A57 towards the M1, then turn onto the A618 signed for Killamarsh. Look for the sign for Wales and follow this into the village. Take a left turn into Manor Road, then 2nd right into Forge Road where the lake is situated.

Description: Two lakes to chose from totalling about 3 acres, The water is deepest towards the centre, but a rod length out will see the best part of 5 foot to fish in. There are plenty of facilities on the site including a cafe and disabled toilets. Many of the 24 pegs are suitable for anglers with disabilities. The new Silver Lake has most species but if you want the larger ghost carp try the bigger lake. Feed and hook pellets are on sale at the shop.

Types of Fish: There are plenty of carp that average 3lb, the largest at around 17lbs. Many crucian to a pound and a half. Good size bream and perch, with roach, ide, rudd and tench present.

Rules/Bans: No keepnets (except during matches). No barbed hooks, no hooks larger than a size 12.
Permitted Baits: maggots, pinkie, squats, caster, blood worm, joker, worm, carp pellets, carp pellet paste, All other baits and ground bait are banned.

Facilities:

Sat Nav:
S26 5RS

Telephone: 01909 773826   **Number of Lakes:** Two

Howbrook Dam.

Westwood New Road, High Green, Sheffield.

Ticket Price: Day Tickets £3.00,
Season tickets available at £20.00. Concessions £12.00.

Directions: Exit the M1 at Junction 36 and head towards Sheffield on the A61. After about a mile you will find the dam on the right. Parking is on the long lay-by.

Description: This dam is about 4 acres in size and has plenty of features to target. Depths vary from 4 feet at one end to over 18 feet at the dam wall. With forty pegs to choose from, many being concrete flags or well built wooden platforms. The dam wall is where I found plenty of tench and carp. Big shoals of bream can be found with the largest fish at around 5lb. The water also has a good head of crucian carp with roach and rudd also present. This venue is not suitable for disabled anglers as access can be tricky. Recently restocked with 1000 rudd, 200 tench and crucian. Take soft hookable pellets for the crucian carp and bream.

Types of Fish: Carp, tench, bream, crucian carp, roach, rudd

Rules/Bans: No night fishing. No bloodworm or joker

Number of Lakes: One

Facilities:

Sat Nav: S35 4FD
to nearby houses.

Telephone: 0777 3482033

Kingsforth Lane Strip Pond

Kingsforth Lane, Thurcroft, Rotherham.

Ticket Price: Day tickets £4.00.

Directions: Come of the M1 at Junction 32 and take the M18. Exit at Junction 1 and turn right heading for Hellaby. As soon as you leave the roundabout turn right. Continue for 1 mile and you should find the pond on your right hand side.

Description: This long strip shaped pond is also know as Cumwell Lane Pond to many locals. It is about an acre in size and tree lined down one side. It has recently been restocked with carp, bream and tench. Plenty of roach and perch are present plus some large carp the biggest being 37lb. There are 22 pegs to chose from, work has been done to make many of them ideal for the disabled angler.

Types of Fish: Tench, bream, carp, perch, roach, ide, gudgeon and a few chub.

56

Rules/Bans: Keepnets are allowed at all times. Barbless hooks only. No hemp, sweetcorn or bloodworm. No groundbait except in a feeder.

Number of Lakes: One

Facilities: ♿ 🅿

Telephone: Mobile 0793 9004170

Sat Nav: S66 8PU to nearest house

Kiveton Hall Farm

Kiveton Lane, Todwick.

Ticket Price: Day tickets £5.00.

Directions: From the M1, Junction 31, head towards Worksop on the A57. At the first set of traffic lights, turn right on to Kiveton Lane and follow the road through Todwick, you will see the entrance to the farm on your left.

Description: Both ponds are a good size with 86 pegs to chose from. With depths of between 4 to 5 feet you catch virtually everywhere especially around the island in one of the lakes. The ponds have a mix of fish but the carp are what most anglers come here for, with the largest reaching around 21lb. This water is well worth a try, but check there is not a match on before you set off.

Types of Fish: Carp to just over 20lb. Barbel to around 7lb. Roach up to 2lb, tench to 4lb, and chub to just under 6lb.

Rules/Bans: No bloodworm, joker, boilies, no ground bait. Keepnets only in matches. No night fishing.

Number of Lakes: Two + new strip pond, full of small carp.

Facilities: 55

Telephone: 0114 2864179   **Sat Nav:** S26 1HJ

35

Kiveton Waters

Hard Lane, Kiverton Park.

Ticket Price: Day tickets £5.00. Concessions £3.00. Under 14's must be accompanied by an adult.

Directions: From the M1, Junction 31, head towards Worksop on the A57. At the first set of traffic lights, turn right on to Kiveton Lane and follow the road to a T-junction. Turn left, then immediate right onto Hard Lane. After about half a mile you will see the lakes on your right.

Description: Kiveton Waters is a British Waterways fishery which opened three years ago. There are three lakes which total approximately 6.5 acres. One of them has been stocked with silver fish only and has 78 pegs, most of which are suitable for the disabled. Try fishing Lake 3, which is the one with an island in the middle. This lake contains the larger carp running to the 15lb mark.

Types of Fish: Tench, carp, roach, rudd, perch and bream.

Number of Lakes: Three

Rules/Bans:

Fishery Rules

- Barbless hooks only, maximum size 12.
- Fishery nets only to be used.
- Ground bait in pole cups and feeders only.
- All feeders must be free running, no bolt rigs.
- No floating baits.
- Fishery feed pellets only to be used, maximum of 2 bags.
- No bait to be thrown in at the end of each session.
- No leaving litter.
- No tins allowed on pegs, all bait must be in bait tubs or bags.
- No washing cat meat in lakes must be done prior to arriving. (only 1 tin per session)
- No children under 14 years without adult supervision.
- Fishing 7am - dusk.

Facilities:

Telephone: 07773 102488   **Sat Nav:** S26 6RP

KJS Fisheries
Station Road, Killamarsh.

Ticket Price: Day tickets are £6.00. OAPs £4.00 mon-fri. Year permits £65.00 which includes Aston Springs and West End fisheries (13 ponds in total).

Directions: From Sheffield head for Mosborough on the A6135. At the main junction in Mosborough turn left, signposted to Killamarsh. Turn right straight after going under a bridge on to Station Road. You will find the fishery at the end of the road.

Description: This well run fishery offers a great variety of sport. You could fish the first and largest pond as you drive in, this is packed with silver fish which can be caught on top during the summer months using maggot or caster. The next lake you come to has more tench and crucian present. Next is the carp lake with fish up to 20lbs. There is also a small stretch of canal.

Types of Fish: Roach, perch, rudd, tench, carp, and bream.

Rules/Bans: No keepnets except on canal section. Barbless hooks only.

Number of Lakes: 4 Lakes, 1 Canal.

Facilities:

26

Telephone: 0114 2470876   **Sat Nav:** S21 1EN

Lewden Spring Fishery

Station Rd, Worsbrough Dale, Barnsley.

SAT NAV S70 4TH

Ticket Price: Adult day ticket £5.00. Under 16's £3.50.
Tickets available on the bank.

Directions: From Junction 36 of the M1 take the A61
heading for Barnsley. When you reach Worsbrough turn
right onto West street (A6100). After about a mile take your
first right onto Station Road. Follow the road down the hill,
when you reach a small bridge, the fishery is on your right.

Description: A very attractive and well run fishery which is
set in woodlands just outside Worsbrough. It has 40 pegs
all with platforms. The best place to catch is close to one of
the large islands or tight to the many margin features.
Meat, pellet or corn all work well for the large carp. Make a
note that they are shut on Tuesdays to let the fish recover
from matches.

Types of Fish: Extensively
stocked with crucian carp,
ide, roach, tench, bream,
rudd and carp upto 24lbs.
Plus a few newly added
chub and barbel.

Number of Lakes: One   **Rules/Bans:**

Facilities: Refreshments at
the weekend between April & Oct

Telephone: 01226 249174

Sat Nav: S70 4TH
to nearby houses

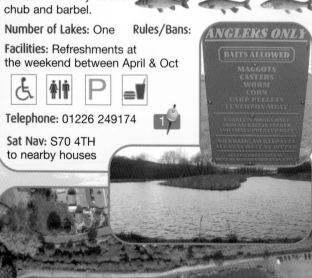

Garbolino Lindholme Lakes

Idle Bank, Sandtoft, Doncaster.

Ticket Price: Day Tickets £6.00. Evenings £1.00 less. Concessions £5.00.

Directions: From the M180, Junction 2 head for Belton. Turn right at the roundabout and follow the road to Sandtoft. When you reach the roundabout in Sandtoft take the second left and continue for nearly a mile. The fishery is signposted on your right.

Description: Lindholme Lakes is situated on over 100 acre of landscaped grounds ,boasting 8 lakes catering for all standards of fishing, from match to specimen to just the lazy days on the bank for pleasure. This makes it one of the biggest in the county but it is still a well run and friendly fishery and not one to be missed. Willows and Laurels Lakes are very similar in size and shape and both have many species present. The Big Lake, which is over 150 years old, is where the bigger carp can be found.

Types of Fish: This water contains a variety of carp many up to 12lb, and a few big ones reaching 29lbs. There are also some very nice tench to 11lb in the Big Lake. Other species include roach, bream, chub, barbel, and pike .

Rules/Bans: No carp in keepnets, no dogs, no joker or bloodworm, barbless hooks only.

Number of Lakes: Eight (503 pegs) **Telephone:** 01427 872905

Facilities:

66

Sat Nav: DN9 1LF   (New tackle shop on-site)

Lodge Farm Fisheries

A638 Great North Rd, Scrooby Top, Doncaster.

SAT DN10 6AX NAV

Ticket Price: Day Tickets £5.00.
Concessions £3.50. Match £6.00.

Directions: Come out of Bawtry heading south on the A638.
Lodge Farm is on the left just before Ranskill.

Description: Five great ponds at this venue with the top pond
having mixed coarse fish with 46 pegs and depths of
around 15 feet. The Lily Pond and Long Pond has mainly
carp, chub, and bream with around 30 pegs each.
Field Pond has 38 pegs with carp , bream, chub and barbel.
Signal Lake has also got carp, bream, chub and a good
head of tench. An excellent cafe has recently opened on
site and is worth a visit.

Types of Fish: Carp, chub, bream, tench, barbel and some
recently introduced ide.

Rules/Bans: No keepnets (except matches),
All nets must be dipped on site, Barbless hooks max size
12, no in line or running method type feeders, no nuts,
boilies, bloodworm or joker. All litter must be taken from site.

Number of Lakes: Five

Facilities: 🚻 ♿ 🅿 🍴   67

Telephone: 0781 5030694   **Sat Nav:** DN10 6AX

Lowfield Lakes

Lowfield Rd, off Station Rd, Bolton Upon Dearne.

SAT NAV S63 8JD

Ticket Price: Day tickets £6.00. Concessions £5.00. Season Ticket £100. Concessions £70.

Directions: The lakes are on the Goldthorpe to Bolton road. When you reach Bolton Upon Dearne, turn left into Station Road. After the railway bridge the road joins with Lowfield Road. The fishery is on the right.

Description: With three lakes to choose from at Lowfields there is plenty of room to fish. The top lake has around 30 pegs with a variation in depth from 7 feet on one side to 4 feet on the other. This lake hold medium to large size carp with a good head of bream and silvers. Corner Pond has 15 pegs and has some large ide, bream and carp. River Side Pond is the match lake which has 30 pegs and holds mainly stockie carp and silver fish.

Types of Fish: Carp are present in all three ponds with some over 21lbs in the top lake, but most are between 2 to 9lb. Tench to 8lb, bream to 9lb, roach and perch between 1 and 2lbs. Ide and a few rudd are also present.

Rules/Bans: No keepnets, except for matches. Barbless hooks only. No night fishing.

Number of Lakes: Three   **Sat Nav:** S63 8JD

Facilities: Refreshments available.

Telephone: 01709 888470 or 07970 171499   45

Loxley Fisheries

Loxley Road, Loxley, Sheffield.

Ticket Price: Adult £5.50. OAPs Mon-Fri £4.50. under 16's £4.

Directions: The fishery is approached off the main Loxley road by taking the second left after passing the Admiral Rodney Pub on your right. The fishery is signposted at the top of the lane, and access is gained through the water treatment plant and the old Marshalls brickworks.
Drive through the works to the car park near the lake.

Description: Pegs 8 or 9 are the favourites, targeting the carp at the side of the lily pads. Surrounded by mature trees and with numerous bank side features this is a very attractive lake. With only 32 pegs to choose from it can get busy on match days leaving only a few pegs for pleasure anglers.
I Like to fish close-in going for the recently stocked barbel. This well run fishery has got to be worth a visit.

Types of Fish: Large carp, roach, tench, perch, chub and barbel.

Rules/Bans: Barbless hooks only, no bloodworm, joker, boilies, or ground bait. Keepnets only in matches.
No night fishing.

Number of Lakes: One

Facilities: **Some** bait sold on site.

Telephone: 07711 429782 or 07860 372807

17

Sat Nav: S6 6SX

Nether Mill Coarse Fishery
Barnsley Road, Penistone.

Ticket Price: Day tickets £5 available on the bank.

Directions: See map.

Description: Nether Mill is a mixed fishery with the emphasis on carp and bream. This one acre lake has three islands in it, and slopes quickly to around 6 feet. The 32 pegs are accessed by a path that runs all the way round making this very friendly for disabled anglers.

Types of Fish: Carp up to 19lb, bream to 7lb. Plenty of other species including roach, perch, tench, rudd, chub and crucian carp.

Rules/Bans: No keepnets, except during matches.
No night fishing, no dogs, no barbed hooks.
Also banned are nuts, cat meat and artificial baits.

Number of Lakes: One   **Sat Nav:** S36 8AD

Facilities:

Telephone: Adam Hinchliff 07770 670042

New Junction Canal
Barnby Dun to West End.

Ticket Price: Day tickets £3.00. Books are valid from April 1st at £19.00. Concessionary rates £12.00 available for OAP's and Juniors.

Directions: All fishing to take place on the west bank, except from Peg 422 to Peg 441 which are on the east bank. All stretches are clearly signposted. When one bank is matched under no circumstances is anyone allowed to fish the opposite bank.

Description: The canal is wide, around 30 metres, with distinct shelves at around 3m from each edge. The top of the ledges is only a few feet deep, but the main channel is around 7 to 10 feet deep making it fishable through winter. There is the odd bush and reed bed to be found creating fish holding features. The main species are Roach and Perch to around 1lb, but eels, chub and bream can put in an appearance if you're in the right place at the right time.

Types of Fish: Bream, perch, roach, chub and eels

Rules/Bans: Barbless hooks only. No vehicles on banks

Number of Lakes: One

Facilities: None

Telephone: 07771 986849

Information kindly supplied by Doncaster & District Angling Association.

The Canal is straight, wide and full of fish.

You'll get a little boat traffic, but it won't disturb your fishing.

There are a few bankside features to be found.

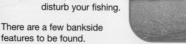

Newbiggin Pond

A616, Lower Newbiggin, Tankersley.

Ticket Price: Day ticket £2.50 Half day £2.00 after 3pm.

Directions: From Junction 36 of the M1 take the A61 heading for Sheffield. At the roundabout turn left onto the A616 heading back to the M1. After about a mile turn left into Park Lane and left again into the fishery carpark.

Description: A very attractive small pond with only 12 pegs, so to avoid disappointment arrive early. Two pegs are suitable for disabled anglers but it can be a bit noisy from traffic on the A616. The depth varies from 3 feet to 6 feet in the middle. There are some good sized carp to 15lb, tench to 4lb and the ide have grown to a healthy 3lbs. Pole fished soft hookable pellets produces good catches of crucian.

Types of Fish: Carp, tench, roach, perch, bream, crucian carp and ide.

Bans/Rules:

Facilities:

Lakes: One

Telephone: 0114 2845424

NEWBIGIN RULES

1. Barbless hooks only (one hook only)
2. No keepnets
3. No bloodworm or joker
4. No litter
5. No live or dead baits
6. Groundbait in feeders and pole pots only
7. No fishing without a licence
8. No fires
9. No fish to be taken away
10. Juveniles under 12 years of age must be accompanied by an adult
11. Landing net must be assembled before fishing

THANK YOU
C.D.A.A

Sat Nav: S35 4LG to nearby Golf Club.

Norwood Cottage Farm Fisheries

Cinder Lane, off Mansfield Rd, Killamarsh, Sheffield.

SAT S21 2AT NAV

Ticket Price: Day tickets are £5.00 on the bank.

Directions: From Junction 31 of the M1, head towards Sheffield. At the first roundabout take a left turn. Keep going past the entrance to Rother Valley. When you reach a small roundabout turn left and go up the hill. You will come across a small turning on your left about a 1/4 of a mile up the hill. Follow the track to the fishery.

Description: This fishery is getting better with age and is already popular with match anglers. Try fishing close up to the islands in the larger pond. This is where I caught most of the dozen or so carp, all of which weighed around 6lbs. Depths vary from one end to the other. I prefer the shallower end near the stock pond, fishing close to the reed beds also produces good weights. Its well worth a visit but pick a still day as their is very little shelter from the wind.

Types of Fish: Carp mainly in the 5-6lb bracket, with a few reaching 15lbs. Bream to 8lb. Tench to 5lb. Plenty of roach and perch to 1lb. Some small ide have been introduced.

Rules/Bans: Barbless hooks only. No floating baits. No keepnets except in matches.

Facilities:

Number of Lakes: Two   **Sat Nav:** S21 2AT

Telephone: Alwyn 0114 2489224

28

Pebley Reservoir

Rotherham Road, Harthill, Sheffield.

Ticket Price: Day Tickets £5.00.
Night fishing by arrangement, £12.00 first night, £10.00 per night for 2 nights. Season tickets £100.00 first year, reduced to £80 for the following year.

Directions: From Junction 30 of the M1, head towards Worksop on the A619. After a mile turn left onto the A618. The reservoir is a mile or so down this road.

Description: A new small pond has been created across the road from the 26-acre main lake. It's been stocked with carp, bream, roach and tench, well worth a visit if you prefer the smaller waters. The main lake is one of the largest waters in the area, with a water depth of between 9 and 24 feet. The shallowest area can be found near the car park, with the deepest being near the dam wall. This is a very attractive lake set in a wooded valley.

Types of Fish: The water carries a good stock of fish, with carp to 30lb+. Plenty of tench to over 9lb, bream to the 15lb mark, roach to 3.3lb. Great pike venue with fish over 27lb. Matches run during the winter months.

Rules/Bans: No fixed rigs. Barbless hooks preferred.
No fish over 3lbs in keepnets

Facilities: None   **Number of Lakes:** Two

Telephone: 07779 813355

Sat Nav: Not available

Pinch Mill Fisheries

Pinch Mill Lane, Whiston, Rotherham.

Ticket Price: Day Tickets £3.50. Two rods £6.00. £50.00 season ticket from the 31st of March (subject to availability)

Directions: Come off the M18 at Junction 1 and head towards Rotherham on the A631. At Worrygoose roundabout turn left and head for Thurcroft on the B6410. After a sharp left hand bend you will come across the fishery, around 200 yards on the left.

Description: There are two lakes to fish and both are tree lined making this a very attractive venue. Both ponds are of a similar size. The first one you come to has 26 pegs and is between 6 and 8 feet in depth. The other pond has 17 pegs and is shallower, around 4 foot. Most pegs are suitable for anglers with disabilities. Both waters are open from dawn till dusk but there is no night fishing.

Types of Fish: Both ponds contain plenty of ide that run to almost 3 pounds, but most average just over the 1 pound mark. There are a few carp present to 22lb, plenty of tench to 4lb, and barbell to 2lb. Good head of perch present.

Rules/Bans: No keepnets, barbless hooks only. No boilies, no trout pellets. Ground bait from pole cup or feeder only.

Number of Lakes: Two   **Sat Nav:** S60 4NJ

Facilities:

Telephone: Rob 07855 312963

Riverside Fishery
Gibbet Hill Lane, Bawtry, Doncaster.

SAT NAV DN10 6BT

Ticket Price: £5.00 per day, £4.00 Concessions
£6.00 Matches, £5.00 Match Concessions

Directions: Take the A614 from Bawtry and head south towards the A1(M). Gibbet Hill Lane is on your left. You will see the entrance straight away on your right.

Description: The lakes here have been completely restocked with a good variety of quality fish. Ricky's Lake has 45 pegs, Strip Lake has 10 pegs, and Sandmartin lake has 20 pegs. They are all similarly stocked with carp to 18lb, crucian and ide to about 1lb and tench to 3lb. All the lakes have a depth of around 5 feet. The river next to the lakes can also be fished.

Types of Fish: Roach, bream, rudd, carp to 18lbs, chub, tench, crucian and ide

  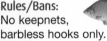

Rules/Bans:
No keepnets,
barbless hooks only.

Number of Lakes: Three

Facilities:

Telephone: 01302 711889   Sat Nav: DN10 6BT

49

Rother Valley Country Park

Mansfield Rd, Wales Bar, Sheffield.

SAT S26 5PQ NAV

Ticket Price: Day ticket £3.50 Concessions £2.50.
Annual season ticket £53.50. Concessions £35.00.

Directions: From the M1 Motorway Junction 31, follow signs to Sheffield city centre. At the first roundabout turn left onto the A618. Rother Valley is on the right after 2 miles.

Description: There are three places to choose from, Northern Lake, Nethermoor Lake and a long stretch of the River Rother. The two lakes contain plenty of perch, roach and carp, but many anglers prefer to fish the river where there has been some large chub caught. The river bank can be overgrown with nettles so be prepared to hack a space for yourself. But trust me it will be worth it.

Types of Fish: Carp, bream, chub, tench, roach, rudd and perch.

Rules/Bans: No ground baiting. Keepnets must not be used during March to June. Barbless hooks only.

Number of Lakes: Two + The River Rother.

Facilities:

24

Telephone: 0114 2471452   **Sat Nav:** S26 5PQ

Roundwood Ponds
Aldwarke Lane, Rotherham.

Ticket Price: £3.50 per day. Concessions £2.50

Directions: From the centre of Rotherham head towards Doncaster on Fitzwilliam Road. When you reach a large roundabout called the Mushroom roundabout, take your first left on to Aldwarke Lane. Continue to the last entrance to Corus steel works and follow the lane down to the ponds.

Description: Two ponds to chose from; one large pond with 30 pegs, and the other fairly small with 20 pegs.
The large pond boasts very good carp up to 33lb with plenty of quality tench. The best place to fish is in the nearest corner of the largest pond. These ponds have recently been taken over and are now improving all the time. Bring some heavy tackle as the fishing is excellent.

Types of Fish: Carp to 33lb, tench to 8lb, pike average around 25lb, roach to 2lb, perch to 4.5lb, bream to 6.5lb, rudd and crucian make up the other species

Rules/Bans: Barbless hooks only, no boilies. no tiger nuts, no braided line, no hooks bigger than size 12.

Number of Lakes: Two   **Sat Nav:** Not available

Facilities: None

Telephone: Six A.M Tackle + Bait. 0114 2873070

Side Farm Fishery

Laughton Common Road, Thurcroft, Rotherham.

SAT NAV S66 9BN

Ticket Price: £5.00 per day. Concessions £4.00

Directions: Come of the M1 at Junction 32 and take the M18. Exit at Junction 1 and turn right heading for Hellaby. As soon as you leave the roundabout turn right. Continue down this road until you reach a T junction at Thurcroft. Turn left onto the B6060 and follow this road through Thurcroft. After nearly a mile the road bends sharply left, after 200 yards you will see the fishery sign on your left.

Description: This new fishery has only been open for two years but is starting to mature nicely. Their are 39 pegs which all have reeds to the side of them. Many carp can be seen moving them while feeding. Depth vary between 3 and 6 foot. Try fishing upto the island that runs the full length of the pond. This can only be reached with a long pole or ideally a feeder rod using sweetcorn on the hook. This is an ideal match venue but has little protection from the wind.

Types of Fish: Carp to 6lb, roach, rudd, perch, bream and ide.

Rules/Bans:

SIDE FARM FISHERY
Tel 07909 758724
FISHERY RULES

1 PERMITTED BAITS
   MAGGOTS
   CASTORS
   CARP PELLETS ONLY (UP TO 6 mm)
   SWEETCORN
   LUNCHEON MEAT (UP TO 1 TIN)
2 GROUNDBAIT IN A FEEDER OR POLE CUP
   UP TO 1 KG
3 BARBLESS HOOKS ONLY (NO MICRO BARBS)
4 MAX HOOK SIZE 12
5 NO KEEPNETS EXCEPT FOR MATCHES
6 ALL NETS ARE PROVIDED BY THE FISHERY
   NO OTHERS ARE ALLOWED
7 PLEASE USE THE LITTER BINS PROVIDED
8 NO DOGS ALLOWED
9 NO CHILDREN UNDER THE AGE OF 15
   UNLESS SUPERVISED BY AN ADULT
ANYONE FOUND BREAKING THESE RULES
   WILL BE BANNED

Number of Lakes: One

Facilities: ♿ P

Sat Nav: S66 9BN

53

Telephone: 07909 758724

Smithies Reservoir
Smithies Lane, Barnsley.

Ticket Price: £3.00 a day. Concessions £1.50.
Under 12's free accompanied by an adult.
Season Tickets £25.00. Concessions £12.50

Directions: From Barnsley head towards Wakefield on the A61. After only half a mile from Barnsley town centre take a left turn into Smithies Lane. Follow the road to the bottom and you will see the water on your righthand side.

Description: The reservoir is in a dip and surrounded by trees. This makes it ideal for fishing on those windy days. Open all year round and with depths averaging 8 feet, this water fishes well in winter. The carp catch well on meat as do the tench. Caster and maggot are ideal for the roach and perch. Good condition pegs make it suitable for disabled anglers

Types of Fish: Lots of bream up to 6lbs, plenty of small carp, but still a few big ones coming in at around 27lb. Tench to 6lb, perch and roach make up the remaining species.

Bans/Rules: Barbless hooks only, no keepnets, except in matches.

Number of Lakes: One   **Sat Nav:** S71 1NL

Facilities:

Telephone: 01226 203090

South Yorkshire Navigation Canal
Doncaster to Long Sandall.

Ticket Price: Day tickets £3.00. Books are valid from April 1st at £19.00. Concessionary rates £12.00 available for OAP's and Juniors.

Doncaster & DAA control full fishing rights on this water wherever it may be sought from below Sprotborough Weir to the railway bridge below Sandall Lock.

Description: The canal runs parallel to the River Don where the river isn't navigable. The water is split into two sections. The largest water runs from above the prison at Doncaster and for a few miles to the railway bridge near Long Sandal Lock. The second section runs from the swing bridge at Barnby Dun for about a mile before it splits to form the New Junction Canal and the Stainforth and Keadby Canal. The width is around 25 metres and depth is around 8 feet down the track. Roach, skimmers, hybrid's, perch and gudgeon are the most common fish, but chub and bream can show occasionally.

Types of Fish:

Facilities: None

Telephone: 07771 986849

44

Information kindly supplied by Doncaster & District Angling Association.

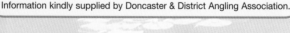

You can park right behind your peg at Long Sandall

Barnby Dun Swing Bridge

The Canal near Barnby Dun. Thorpe Marsh Power Station in the background.

Straight Mile Fishery
Common Road, Brampton, near Dinnington.

SAT S25 4AH NAV

Ticket Price: Day ticket £5.00 at the weekend.
£4.00 during the week.

Directions: From the M1 Motorway Junction 31 take the A57 to Worksop. Turn left at the first set of traffic lights. After about half a mile turn left again into Pocket Handkerchief Lane. At the end of the lane turn left and the fishery is on your left hand side.

Description: The lake is made up of four strips separated by three islands, with plenty of features to target. You will catch in the middle, near the islands or close in. This is an all year round fishery with 100lb nets recorded. This is one of the largest match angling fisheries in the area , boasting 90 pegs. The venues prolific roach stocks, mean that bites are rarely hard to come by.

Types of Fish: Carp, bream, chub, barbel, roach.

Rules/Bans: Barbless hooks only.
Juniors Must be accompanied by an adult.

Facilities:

Number of Lakes: One   **Sat Nav:** S25 4AH   54

Telephone: 01909 561663

Tinkers Pond

Woodstock Road, Barnsley.

Ticket Price: Day Tickets £3.00, Concessions at £1.50. Available on the bank.

Directions: From Barnsley city centre head towards Huddersfield on the A635. When you pass Barnsley College turn right on to Woodstock Road. Follow the road to the end, go under the railway bridge, and you will find the ponds on your right.

Description: There are two very similar ponds to choose from, except for the depths. The first water known as Top Pond ranges between 4 feet and 12 feet at its deepest. The other pond coincidentally called Bottom Pond, is much shallower reaching only 6 feet. I found fishing close-in produced good bites every time (mostly tench). This fishery has specially designed pegs for wheelchair anglers.

Types of Fish: Carp averaging 4lb with the biggest around 20lb. Tench go to 6lb. Bream at 4lb. Plenty of roach (2½lb) and perch 4lb.

Rules/Bans: Keepnets to be used only during matches. Barbless hooks only.

Number of Lakes: Two

Sat Nav: S75 1DX
to nearest house

Facilities:

Telephone: 01226 203090

Bottom Pond

56

Triangs Fishery
Tythe Farm, Kirton Lane, Thorne.

Ticket Price: Day Ticket £5.00. 7 am to an hour before dusk.

Directions: From the M180 Junction 1, take the A614 towards Thorne. Turn left just before the canal flyover and head towards Stainforth. Turn right just after crossing the railway lines into Kirton Lane. You need to open the gates to cross back over the railway line (ring from phone at side of track first). The fishery is few hundred yards on your left.

Description: Four excellent waters here. Kingfisher is for year book holders only, but there is plenty of room on the other lakes. Heron pool with 20 pegs is stuffed with a variety of species but the tench do seem to be the dominant fish. Willow ponds depths vary from 5 feet to 10 feet and is stocked mainly with carp. There is a small island which when fished close to gives the best results.

Types of Fish: Carp to 25lb, tench to 5lb, chub, bream, roach, crucian, perch, rudd and ide.

Rules/Bans: No ground bait, boilies, nuts, cat or dog food. No night fishing. Under 14s must be accompanied by an adult. No keepnets, barbless hooks only.

Number of Lakes: Four   **Sat Nav:** DN8 5RJ

Facilities: P ♿

Telephone: 01405 816402 or 07890 167407

69

Tyram Hall Fishery
Moor Dike Road, Hatfield Woodhouse.

SAT NAV DN7 6DR

Ticket Price: Day tickets Carp Lake £6.00 upto 3 rods. 24hr £12.   Coarse Lake £5.00. £2.00 per extra rod.

Directions: Heading South on the A18, take the A614 to Bawtry. Go through Hatfield Woodhouse and take a left to the carpark.

Description: This popular fishery has four ponds and offers excellent sport all year round. The carp lake has some very large fish around the 30lb mark. The main coarse lake has plenty of silver fish, and either pole or feeder fishing will catch good net weights. There are some large pike at this fishery, weights up to 25lb have been landed. Try the smallest lake called Tench Lake. It is usually the quietest, but as the name suggests there are plenty of tench to target.

Types of Fish: The Coarse lake has roach, perch, tench and bream. Many types of carp in the carp lake. A few large pike.

Rules/Bans: No keepnets, barbless hooks only. dawn till dusk fishing.

Number of Lakes: Four   **Sat Nav:** DN7 6DR

Facilities:

Telephone: 01302 840886

65

Underbank Reservoir

Underbank Reservoir, Stocksbridge.

SAT NAV S36 1AU

Ticket Price: Day tickets £4.00. per rod
Ring for information about pike fishing.

Directions: From Sheffield head towards Stocksbridge on the A616. You can't miss the reservoir just on the edge of Stocksbridge.

Description: Like most reservoirs in South Yorkshire it has plenty of depth, which provides anglers with good all year round fishing. If you like pike fishing then this is the water for you. Underbank also has a healthy stock of silver fish that are great sport. Many anglers come in the early morning to catch the bream that feed at that time. A big favourite for piking from October to March

Types of Fish: Plenty of pike plus perch and roach to a pound, lots of carp, bream and tench.

Rules/Bans: All necessary equipment required for pike fishing

Number of Lakes: One

Facilities: None

Sat Nav: S36 1AU
to the nearest houses.

Telephone: 07976 797158

Westwood Reservoir

Downland Avenue, High Green, Sheffield.

Ticket Price: Day Tickets £3.00.
Year permits £20.00 starting in March, concessions £12.00

Directions: From the M1 Junction 36, head towards Sheffield on the A61. When you reach High Green turn left on to Wortley Road. After a short distance turn left into Westwood Road. Turn next right into Downland Avenue and follow this road to the bottom where you will find the reservoir.

Description: This is an excellent all year round venue. Great for roach in the colder months. Like a lot of reservoirs this one is very deep and can reach over 19 feet in places. A great water to fish with plenty of species to target, however it has only got 40 pegs and can get busy especially on match days. A few pegs near to the car park are suitable for the disabled angler as further along the bank it becomes fairly steep.

Types of Fish: The largest bream are just under 6lb. There are also plenty of chub present up to 5lb. The other main species are carp which reach 21lb. Tench nearing 5lb. Plenty of barbel have recently been stocked.

Rules/Bans: No keepnets, barbless hooks only. No bloodworm or joker.

Number of Lakes: One   **Sat Nav:** S35 4DE

Facilities:

Telephone: 0114 2845424

West End Fisheries

Boiley Lane, Killamarsh, Sheffield.

Ticket Price: £6.00 per day. OAPs £4.00 mon-fri.
Year permits £65.00 which includes KJS and Aston Springs fisheries (13 ponds in total).

Directions: At the main shopping area in Killamarsh turn up Bridge St, and turn right at the Nags Head public house. Keep going on this road till you get to the West End pub where you turn right, then immediately left onto Boiley Lane. Follow the track to an old railway bridge, turn right into the car park.

Description: This fishery has been well stocked with carp, roach, rudd, bream and tench. The main lake has 50 pegs, some situated in an island in the middle of the lake. Targeting these small islands gives you the best chance of catching the numerous carp present. A new lake with 22 pegs has been built for both pleasure and match fishing.

Types of Fish: Carp, rudd, bream, tench, and roach.

Rules/Bans: Barbless hooks only. No keepnets. All anglers must use a landing net. No ground bait except in a cup or feeder. Under 16's must be accompanied by an adult.

Number of Lakes: Three.

Facilities: [P] [🍔🥤] [🚻] Cafe open in summer months

Telephone: 0114 2470876   **Sat Nav:** S21 1AG

61

Willow Garth Ponds

Shaftholme Road, Arksey, Doncaster.

Ticket Price: Day tickets are £4.00. Juniors £3.00. Evenings £3.00 / £2.00. Night fishing £8.00.

Directions: Head towards Bentley on the A19. Turn right when you see the sign post for Arksey. Follow this road until you see a turn on to Shaftholme Lane. Cross over the railway line into Shaftholme Road. You will see the fishery on your right.

Description: This water is open throughout the year and does get busy during the summer months. Both lakes have plenty of features to fish. The carp and tench are the prominent species with the carp reaching 30lbs. Try hair-rigged boilies or luncheon meat for these large carp. In the summer months give floating crust or dog biscuit a go. Watch out while float fishing, as their are a few pike in these ponds.

Types of Fish: Tench, roach, rudd, carp, crucian and pike.

Number of Lakes: Two

Rules/Bans: No keepnets, barbless hooks only.

Facilities:

Telephone: 01302 563728

47

Sat Nav: Not available

Wire Mill Dam Fishery
Whiteley Wood Road, Sheffield.

Ticket Price: Day Tickets £3.50. Concessions £2.50
After 4pm £2.00. Year Permits £30. Concessions £20.

Directions: From the centre of Sheffield take the A625 (Ecclesall Road). Turn right on to Knowle Lane after passing the Prince of Wales Pub. Continue up Knowle Lane and turn right 600 metres past the Hammer and Pincers Pub. Follow the road for about 1 mile and you will find the dam and car park on your left.

Description: Great for beginners with plenty of roach, perch, tench, and a good head of crucian carp. It is quite shallow at only 4 feet at its deepest. This dam is full of fish and during the summer months maggot or sweet corn will catch all day long. Try feeder fishing to the far bank where many of the larger fish hold up. Use luncheon meat hair rigged for the numerous tench that reach 7lb. This tactic also works for the carp which reach 16lbs. The high quality roach and perch also makes this water one of the best winter fishing venues in the area.

Types of Fish: Carp, roach, perch, tench, bream, crucian carp and golden orfe.

Rules/Bans: Barbless hooks only, no keepnets except in matches, no night fishing. Ground bait in pole cup or feeder only. No floating baits.

Number of Lakes: One   **Telephone:** 07809 172872

Facilities: P   ♿   Sat Nav: S11 7FF   21

63

Wombwell Dam
Woodhead Lane, Wombwell, Barnsley.

Ticket Price: Day ticket £5.00 Concessions £4.00 £60.00 for the year.

Directions: From Junction 36 of the M1, take the A6095 signposted Wombwell. After about 3 miles, at the fifth roundabout turn left onto Woodhead Lane. After a hundred yards turn right onto a dirt track and follow this down to the carpark. The waters are a short walk through the trees.

Description: There are two waters to fish at Wombwell Dam. The main dam depth varies between 3 and 24 feet, with plenty of carp over 10lb. The smaller pond contains crucian carp and tench. Both are surrounded by woodland making this a very attractive place to fish.

Types of Fish: Carp, bream, tench, roach, and perch.

Rules/Bans: Barbless hooks only. Keepnets are banned during the close season.

Number of Lakes: Two

Sat Nav: Not available

Facilities: None

Telephone: 01226 292579

36

Woodhouse Grange

Woodhouse Grange Lakes, Hatfield Woodhouse.

SAT NAV DN7 6DU

Ticket Price: Day tickets £6.00 from cafe.
Matches £6.00 for 5 hours, £7.00 for 6 hours.

Directions: From Bawtry head north on the A614.
Go through Blaxton and you will find the fishery on your right just before you reach Hatfield Woodhouse.

Description: There are six waters to choose from. Heron, Cobbie and Kingfisher lakes house the heavier carp to 30lbs. Ghost Lake has plenty of silver fish with carp to 12lb and Kennel Lake which is the largest with 37 pegs has tench to 9lb. These are excellent ponds with plenty of quality fish to target. Everyone seemed to be catching on the day I went, fishing at a poles length with a white maggot worked for me. Also try feeder fishing large pellets or corn during the summer months.

Types of Fish: Roach, perch, bream, carp, crucian, rudd, ide and tench.

Rules/Bans: No bloodworm or joker, no hempseed or tares, no boilies or nuts, no method feeder. Barbless 12 max hooks. No keepnets. Ground baits in small feeder or pole cup.

Number of Lakes: Six   **Sat Nav:** DN7 6DU

Facilities:

Telephone: 07702 189657 or 07802 518612

71

Woodland Farm Fisheries
Ward Lane, Barlborough.

SAT S43 4JD NAV

Ticket Price: Day tickets £5.00.
OAP's juniors £4.00.

Direction: From Sheffield head for Junction 30 of the M1.
Just before the junction turn left, sign posted Barlborough
Village. Ward Lane is on the left when you reach the shops.
Follow the lane to the bottom where you will find the fishery.

Description: The fishery has something for everyone, with 82
pegs over four lakes there's plenty for match, pleasure and
specimen anglers. Ice House Lake and Bluebell Lake
contain the larger fish with carp to 26lbs. Island Pond holds
carp to around 7lb with roach, orfe, ide, and skimmers.
Kingfisher Lake has a mixture of silver fish and carp up to
15lb.

Types of Fish: Carp, rudd, roach, bream, ide, orfe.

Rules/Bans: Keepnets only in matches.
No night fishing. Barbless hooks only

Number of Lakes: Four

Facilities:

Sat Nav: S43 4JD
to the top of the lane.

59

Telephone: 0114 2653541 or 07771 851185

Worsbrough Canal

West Street, Worsbrough, Barnsley.

Ticket Price: £3.00 for the day.
OAPs or under 16s - £2.00.

Directions: From the M1, Junction 36, take the A61 and head towards Barnsley. After passing the Button Mill Pub, at the next set of traffic lights, turn right onto the B6100. The canal is on the righthand side, opposite the Wharfe pub.

Description: At just over five foot deep this canal has some overhanging trees and reed beds. This well kept stretch of canal is about 260 yards long and has 45 pegs. The carp have grown and now reach double figures. Most anglers pole fish this stretch of canal for the large head of roach. Good stock of crucians which like sweetcorn and pellet.

Types of Fish: Carp to about 10lb, chub to 4lb, bream and tench to 5lb, plenty of crucian to around 1lb, and lots of roach, perch and rudd.

Rules/Bans: Barbless hooks only, no keepnets, except in matches.

Number of Lakes: One

Facilities: None

Sat Nav: S70 5PF to nearest houses.

Telephone: 01226 289714 mobile 0795 8683015

Worsbrough Reservoir

A61, Sheffield Road, Barnsley.

Ticket Price: Day tickets are £3.00 on the bank.
Season tickets £25.00. £12.50 Concessions.

Directions: Coming from Barnsley take the A61 south. When you get to Worsbrough go through a set of traffic lights and turn right into Worsbrough Mill Country Park, across the road from the Button Mill pub.

Description: There are 80 pegs to fish at Worsbrough, with trees to one side and stone banks to the other. The depths vary from shallows to around 15 feet at the dam head. This reservoir is fished by top match anglers all year round. Parking is pay and display in the carpark.

Types of Fish: There are a lot of bream to the 5lb mark, roach to 2lb, lots of big perch. You can also find pike here with many to 14lbs in weight, plus some good quality tench. Recently re-stocked with carp now weighing upto 14lb.

Rules/Bans: No carp in keepnets, free running method feeder only. No bloodworm, joker or nuts.

Number of Lakes: One   **Sat Nav:** S70 5LL

Facilities:

Telephone: 01226 203090

BillyClarkeFishingTackle
Established 1918

Official Fox, Shimano & Daiwa Distributor

77-81 Alderson Road, Sheffield, S2 4UB. (off London Road & Bramall Lane)

T. 0114 255 1145   T/F. 0114 258 7575
Open 9am - 5.30pm Monday - Saturday
www.billyclarke.co.uk
E. sales@billyclarke.co.uk

Interest free credit available subject to status

Shop online at: **www.billyclarke.co.uk**

Rivers

River Dearne
Denaby Main

Ticket Price: Day tickets and season permits available, ring for details.

Directions: From the A1 follow the signs for the Denaby Main, carry on through Denaby Main up to the roundabout, go right at the roundabout over the River Don and canal and turn right at the ATS garage onto Pastures Road. Carry on down the road past the Pasture Lodge Motel, go over the River Dearne bridge

then turn immediately right into the car park. Finally go over the stile and you are on the banks of the River Dearne.

Description: This stretch of the River Dearne is run by the Denaby Miners Welfare Angling Club and comprises of 60 pegs from the Pastures Road Bridge to the confluence with the River Don at Denaby Main. Twenty species of fish have been recorded in the last few years. The dominant fish have been skimmers, hybrid's, roach, chub, perch, gudgeon, and dace. Chub to 3lb are a regular size catch. The highest pleasure fishing weight record is 49lbs 15oz consisting of 184 roach and a single skimmer caught with a waggler and caster.

Types of Fish: Bream, roach, perch, chub, dace, gudgeon and carp.

Telephone:
01709 864037

1

Information kindly supplied by the Denaby Miners Welfare A.C.

River Don

Doncaster, Hexthorpe and Sprotborough.

Ticket Price: Day ticket £3.00
Books are valid from April 1st at £19.00
Concessionary rates £12.00 available for OAP's and
Juniors.

Directions:

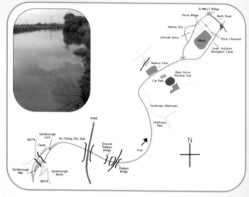

Description: Doncaster & D.A.A. control the fishing rights on
the Don from Sprotborough Weir and downstream to
Crimpsall Sluice near Doncaster Prison.

The river is deep, up to 15 feet down the centre, with a
width of around 30 metres. Because of the depth, fish can
be caught all year round. In fact it's not uncommon for big
bags on some of the colder winter days.

At usual level the river is slow, almost still at times, but be
careful when it's been raining. Because the banks are steep
the river is prone to rising quickly. Even a foot of extra water
will make the river very difficult to fish.

The main species to be caught are roach, skimmers, perch,
barbel and chub, but dace, bream, pike, eels and even carp
can be found.

The barbel average around 3 to 5 lbs but bigger fish have
been caught and they're getting bigger every year.

Bags of small fish can top 20lbs on a good day, but 10lbs is
still a good catch.

River Don, Hexthorpe

Sprotborough Weir

Eden Grove, Hexthorpe

Methods:

One of the great things about the River Don is that fish can be caught on the pole, stick float, waggler, topper, slider, groundbait feeder, bomb and almost any method you can think of. For the barbel try meat or pellet on the hook over a bed of hemp. If you can find a patch of gravel the barbel will find you.

For the chub, look for pegs with overhanging trees or a crease in the current. The classic combination of hemp and caster should do the trick.

For the roach and skimmer you can loose feed, but the depth means that is usually better to fish over a bed of groundbait. The pole is the obvious choice when the river is at normal level, but a float on running line is better when the river is up 6 inches or so. Try pinkies, maggots or caster.

Rigs:

If you're after the barbel or chub they can be had on the usual feeder or bomb setups, but don't discount the stick float or waggler. Try running a heavy float with plenty of shot down the line. You can drag up to a couple of feet along the bottom to slow the bait down as most pegs are snag free with a sandy bottom. Hooklengths should be around at least 3 to 4lb. Hooks should suit your bait size, but a size 14 will give you plenty of leverage should you hook a big 'un. The roach and skimmers can be a little cute, so you'll have to scale your rigs down, whether you use the pole or running line. Hooklengths as light as 1lb (0.006) are sometimes the only way you can get bites.

Rules/Bans:

No fires or camping allowed.
No night fishing. No live baits.
No cars or motorcycles allowed
on banks. No wasp grub.
Bloodworm and joker is only
allowed between Oct and March.
No litter to be left on banks.
Keep to recognised footpath.
Close all gates.

Types of Fish: Roach, perch, barbel and chub, bream, pike, eels and carp

Telephone: 07771 986849

Information kindly supplied by Doncaster & District Angling Association.

River Idle
Bawtry. Newington. Mission.

Ticket Price: Fishing is free on the Bawtry stretch of the Idle. At Newington and Mission; day tickets are available.

Directions: Bawtry. Leave the A1 and take the A631 (Bawtry Rd) signposted Bawtry. Proceed through High Street and turn left onto Wharf Street. Park and take the footpath under the viaduct and follow this path to the left which will take you to the river.
Newington.
From Bawtry take the A164 heading to Finningley. When you reach Newington turn right at the Ship Inn and park.
Mission.

From Newington take Bawtry Road and after a mile or so you will reach Mission. Drive through the village and turn right into River Lane. Follow the lane to the river.

Description: The river in most places is between 12 and 20 feet wide, with depths from 4 to 7 feet. The water runs at an easy pace and I found using a stick float with a single red maggot worked well, but to avoid the gudgeon try a bit of corn. There's a very good stock of silver fish with roach over two pounds. Good size bream have been caught some to six pounds. Chub and perch make up the other dominant species. This river is also great for piking with some old ones reaching twenty pounds.

Types of Fish: Pike, roach, perch, chub, bream, gudgeon and dace.

74

River Rother
Catcliffe, Sheffield.

Ticket Price: Day ticket £2.00. Adult season tickets £10.00. OAP's and children under 16 £5.00. Children under 12 can fish for free if accompanied by an adult who is also fishing.

Directions: It is easy to find by car just off the M1 motorway, Junction 33, via the Sheffield Parkway to the village of Catcliffe. The river runs alongside Orgreave Road, with free parking at both ends of the fishery via The Plough public house.

Description: Who would have thought that the once most polluted river in the country a few years ago would have turned out to be a vastly improving fishery? We are talking about the Rother in Catcliffe. Catcliffe, Brinsworth and Treeton Anglers Alliance have control of a mile of river at Catcliffe, and believe me it produces some very good fish. Big perch the best up to now being a 4 pounder taken by Mick Kitchin in a match when he had eight perch for 21 pounds. There are also some very good chub, up to 5 pounds, with a few 2 pound roach. Some very good barbel, carp and pike, dace and gudgeon, also trout up to 4 pounds. There are 50 platforms, 23 of these are 4 foot wide and 5 foot long. These are ideal for the disabled angler. The fishery offers many good aspects of fishing. Its diversity offers good sport to the many different types of fishing, with some very deep slow glides to faster shallow swims, making it ideal for float or ledger fishing, or spinning for pike, perch and trout.

Types of Fish: Pike, roach, perch, chub, carp, trout and recently a few 12lb barbel have been caught .

Facilities:

P ♿

Telephone:
07774 884946

4

Information kindly supplied by Clive Nuttall Secretary of Catcliffe, Brinsworth, Treeton Anglers Alliance.

River Torne
Epworth Road Bridge to Pilfrey Bridge.

Ticket Price: Day ticket £3.00. Books are valid from April 1st at £19.00. Concessionary rates £12.00 available for OAP's and Juniors.

Directions: Epworth Road Bridge to Pilfrey Bridge on the A18 - a stretch of about 15 miles. Access may be gained at various road bridges.

IMPORTANT NOTICE

The River Torne Epworth Bridge to Belton Bridge

Please refer to the map. There is no vehicular access from Belton Bridge upstream past Dippings Farm towards Epworth Road Bridge. Anglers must park at Belton Bridge and walk upstream. Alternatively, anglers may drive downstream from Epworth Bridge, but not past Dippings Farm. Anglers using this

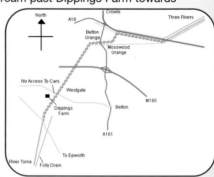

water must park off the track to allow the safe passage of farm vehicles and lorries. This track is Private Property. Please respect the owners wishes and the agreements that the Association has made with the owners.

Description: Technically this section is in North Lincolnshire. The river is more of a drain than a river and is close to the border with South Yorkshire. It's only around 13 metres wide but there is a little variety where sections of rushes extend into the water. Depth is around 4 or 5 feet. In summer the river can be slow, weedy and clear, but in winter the water is usually coloured due to water being pumped off the fields. Roach are the predominant species, but the river is probably most famous for its pike population. Plenty of fish to over 20lbs are caught every year and jacks to mid singles are commonplace.

The River Torne at Belton Grange.

The River Torne near Mosswood Grange

Methods: For the pike deadbaits are king, but spinning comes a very close second.

Caster, punched bread or pinkie are the key baits for the roach. Hemp and tares can be great if you find big shoal of roach.

Pole fishing with a long line is often best but be careful of spooking the fish in the clear water.

Small amounts of loose feed should be fed regularly. If bites don't come quickly try feeding and fishing further downstream to draw the fish up, then bring them up the river by feeding back at your starting point

Rigs: Fish light rigs with No.11 shot or even better, No.9 leads spread out so that the bait falls naturally through the water at the same speed as your loose feed.

Many of your bites from the roach will come on the drop and will be sharp, so be alert.

Experiment with different feeding patterns until the bites become easier to hit.

Don't go too light with the lines because of the weed. Try around 1.5 to 2lbs with hooks around a size 22.

Types of Fish: Pike, roach, perch, tench, chub, and eels.

Rules/Bans:
No fires or camping allowed.
No night fishing. No livebaits.
No cars or motorcycles allowed
on banks. No wasp grub.
Bloodworm and joker is only
allowed between Oct and March.
No litter to be left on banks.
Keep to recognised footpath.
Close all gates.

Telephone: 07771 986849

Information kindly supplied by Doncaster & District Angling Association.

I have tried to ensure the accuracy of this guide but things do change very quickly so if you know of any inaccuracies or any fisheries I have not included I would be grateful if you could fill out and return the form at the back of the guide
Lastly if you have or know of a pond or small lake for sale I would be very interested. Contact me (Chris) on 07809 172872

South Yorkshire Tackle Shops

Alan's Fishing Tackle, 111 Main St, Bramley, Rotherham, S66 2SE.	01709 702454
Bag-Up Angling Supplies, 16d Station Rd, Chapeltown, S35 2XH	0114 2466670
Bankside Tackle + Bait, 2 Balmoral Rd, Sheffield, S13 7QG.	0114 2692483
Barries Fishing tackle, 14 King Avenue, Doncaster. DN11 0PG.	01302 863832
Bennetts Of Sheffield Ltd, 1 Stanley St, Sheffield, S3 8JP.	0114 2756756
Billy Clarke, 77-81 Alderson Rd, Sheffield, S2 4UB.	**0114 2551145**
Carrilon UK, Hawks Nest, Great North Rd, Doncaster DN10 6AB.	01302 719933
Climax Fishing Tackle Ltd, 2 Stubley Hollow, Dronfield. S18 1PP	**01246 291155**
Cookes Angling Supplies, 3 Greasborough Rd, Rotherham.	01709 820579
Dave Parkes Fishing Tackle, 46 Westgate, Rotherham, S60 1AS.	01709 363085
Dawson's Of Hillsborough, 70-72 Holme Lane, Sheffield, S6 4JW.	0114 2812178
Decathlon, Eyre St, Sheffield, S1 4QZ.	0114 2298190
Doncaster Angling Centre, 207 Carr House Rd, Doncaster.	01302 363629
First For Fishing, 10 Fieldside, Thorne, Doncaster. DN8 4BQ	01405 818277
Fishing Republic, Snape Hill Rd, Darfield, Barnsley, S73 9JU.	01226 752300
Fishing Republic, 12 Stoke Street, Attercliffe, Sheffield. S9 3QD	0114 2441339
Kingfisher Angling Centre, 148 High St, Bentley, Doncaster, DN5 0AT.	01302 874888
High Green Angling Centre, 1 Wortley Rd, Sheffield S35 4LQ.	0114 2845176
Ian's Fishing Tackle Shop, 303 Prince Of Wales Rd, Sheffield.	0114 2531533
Kerfoot's Fishing Tackle, 6 Southey Green Rd, Sheffield, S5 8GW.	0114 2313265
Killamarsh Angling Supplies, 120 Sheffield Rd, Killamarsh, S21 1EB	0114 2514936
Mosborough Tackle Box, 38b High St, Sheffield, S19 5AE.	0114 2510664
Oaks Lane Angling Centre, 99 Oaks Lane, Rotherham, S61 3BA	01709 559070
Parkgate Angling Centre, 19 Broad St, Parkgate, Rotherham, S62 6DX.	01709 527297
Pauls Fishing Tackle Centre, Doncaster Rd, Doncaster DN12 4HU.	01709 862558
Peg 31, Laughton Rd, Dinnington, Sheffield, S25 2PT.	01909 562552
R & R Sports, 40 High St, Bawtry, Doncaster, DN10 6JE.	01302 711130
Pete's Fishing Tackle, 65 Main St, Mexborough, S64 9ND.	01709 581715
Scawthorpe Fishing, 13 Crossland Way, Doncaster, DN5 9EX.	01302 789977
Six A.M Tackle + Bait, 82 Worksop Rd, Swallownest, Sheffield.	0114 2873070
Slippery Suckers, 30 Queens Drive, Barnsley, S72 8PB.	01226 711512
Stainforth Angling Ctr, 24 Silver St, Stainforth, Doncaster DN7 5AH.	01302 846623
Supabait, Clifton Lane, Clifton, Doncaster, DN12 2AL.	01709 863341
Tackle 2 Fish, Unit 27, Penistone Rd Trading Estate, Sheffield, S6 2FL	**0114 2323696**
Tackle Box, 7 Doncaster Rd, Barnsley, S70 1TH.	01226 247131
Tardis Tackle, 116A Brampton Rd, Wath-upon-Dearne S63 6AW	01709 879299
Tardis Tackle Angling Centre, 4 Sicey Ave, Sheffield.	0114 2436655
Thorne Pet & Angling, 5 The Green, Thorne, Doncaster, DN8 5AP.	01405 814056
Tight Lines Tackle, Glenshiel, Birley Moor Rd, Sheffield S12 4WG.	0114 2658178
Tigra Fishing Tackle, 14-15 Shopping Centre, Bellows Rd, Rawmarsh	01709 719252
Tony's Tackle, 10 Lidget Lane, Thurnscoe, Rotherham S63 0BU.	01709 880065
Intake Angling Supplies, 27a Mansfield Rd, Sheffield S12 2AE.	0114 2649664
Wickersley Angling Centre, 2-4 Hellaby Ind Est, Rotherham, S66 8HR	01709 540998
Wombwell Angling Ctr, 25 Barnsley Rd, Barnsley S73 8HT.	01226 750659
Woodlands Angling, 232 Great North Rd, Doncaster, DN6 7HR	01302 728876
Woodseats Angling, 625 Chesterfield Rd, Sheffield S8 0RX.	0114 2585133

I N D E X

page no.

Readers Special Offer

Any book for £7.99 each.	Saving £1.00
Any 2 books £7.50 each - total £15.00	Saving £2.98
Any 3 books £6.99 each - total £20.97	Saving £6.00
Any 4 books £5.99 each - total £23.96	Saving £12.00
All 5 books £4.99 each - total £24.95	**Saving £20.00**

HOW TO ORDER

Please enter your selection and quantity of books you require.

- ☐ Fish-it Lincolnshire
- ☐ Fish-it3 East Yorkshire
- ☐ Fish-it5 North Yorkshire
- ☐ Fish-it2 South Yorkshire
- ☐ Fish-it4 West Yorkshire
- ☐ All five books

Name..

Address..

....

....

Phone No..

Please add £2.00 to cover postage +packing.

I enclose a cheque for £..............

Please make cheques payable to: ARC PUBLISHING AND PRINT

Please send your completed form together with your cheque/postal order to:
ARC PUBLISHING, 166 KNOWLE LANE, SHEFFIELD, S11 9SJ.

New Fishery / Fishery Update Form

New Fishery ☐

Update to Fishery ☐

Fishery Name

Fishery Address

Post code

Contact Name

Telephone / Fax

Adult Day Ticket Price £ | concession OAP'S £

Fish Species and Weights

Brief Description

Please return this form to:
Arc Publishing and Print
166 Knowle Lane
Sheffield S11 9SJ

Please e-mail or post a colour photo for inclusion in the next publication.